WINSTON YOUNG

Emotional Mastery

First edition

This book was professionally typeset on Reedsy.
Find out more at reedsy.com

Contents

Chapter 1: The Foundation of Emotional Intelligence

Understanding and Recognizing Your Emotions

We live in a world driven by data, logic, and information, but what often gets overlooked is the role our emotions play in shaping our everyday decisions and interactions in our life. Consider a heated argument with a colleague at work. Later, you might realize that your frustration wasn't necessarily about the disagreement itself but about feeling disrespected. Emotional intelligence helps you uncover the layers beneath these emotions, so you can better understand yourself and the world around you.

The Overwhelmed Manager

Let's take the example of Sarah, a mid-level manager who finds herself snapping at her team during a high-pressure project. While her initial thought is that the stress of the looming deadline is making her irritable, upon reflection, Sarah realizes that the real issue is her fear of being perceived as incompetent. She wants to prove herself but hasn't communicated her concerns effectively. By understanding her own emotional drivers, Sarah can address her stress more productively and support her team without conflict.

Emotional intelligence, or EQ, is not about eliminating emotion but learning to manage and harness it. As we delve into this chapter, you'll discover how becoming emotionally aware is the key to mastering your emotional world.

What is Emotional Intelligence?

Emotional intelligence refers to your ability to perceive, control, and evaluate emotions—both in yourself and others. The concept gained mainstream recognition through psychologist Daniel Goleman's work, who identified EQ as equally, if not more, important than IQ when it comes to life success. Emotional intelligence touches every aspect of our lives—from how we communicate and handle stress to how we motivate ourselves and build relationships.

Think about the difference between two leaders: One reacts impulsively to challenges, driven by frustration, while the other stays calm, weighs the options, and responds thoughtfully. The second leader has high emotional intelligence and uses it to create an environment of trust and respect.

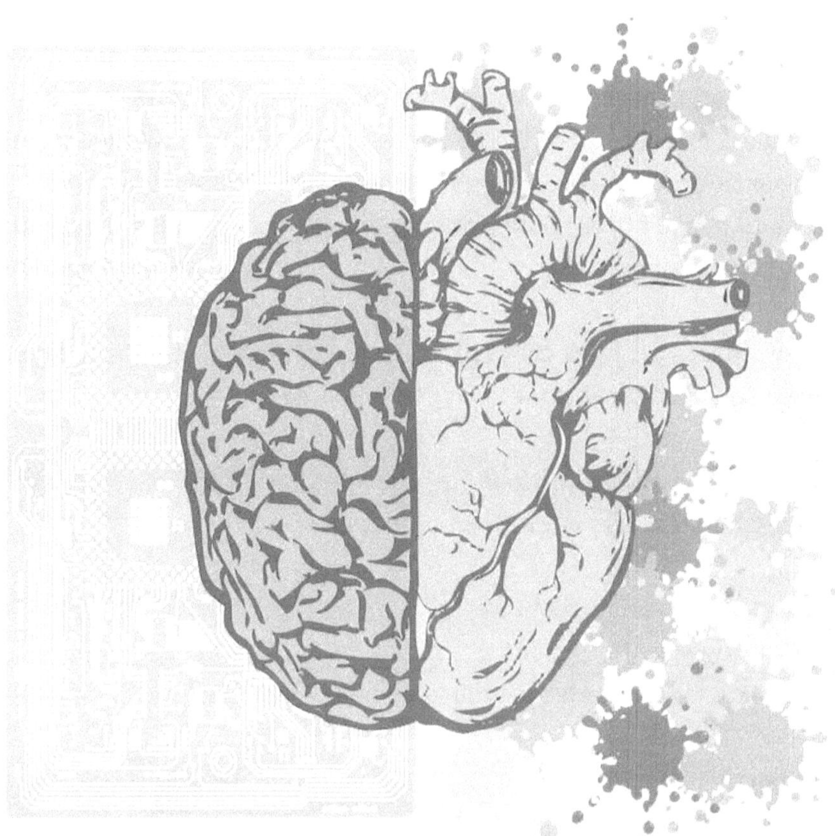

The Power of Self-Awareness

Self-awareness is the foundation of emotional intelligence. It involves recognizing your emotions, understanding where they come from, and acknowledging how they impact your thoughts and actions. This level of self-awareness helps you make intentional choices rather than reacting impulsively.

Here's an Example:

The Athlete and Self-Awareness

Consider a professional athlete who loses a game and feels overwhelmed with frustration. If they lack self-awareness, they might lash out at teammates, the coach or sulk, letting the emotion consume them. However, with self-awareness, the athlete would pause and realize that the frustration isn't solely about losing—it's tied to deeper fears, like letting down their team or failing in front of fans. This insight allows them to address the true root of the emotion, and instead of reacting negatively, they use the frustration as motivation to improve.

Self-awareness isn't just about naming your emotions. It's about digging deeper and understanding the "why" behind them.

Exercise: The Emotional Check-In
Take 5 minutes every day to practice the emotional check-in:

- What am I feeling right now?
- What triggered this emotion?
- How are my actions being influenced by this emotion?

By regularly reflecting on your emotions, you build the skill of recognizing emotional patterns and triggers, leading to more thoughtful responses.

Emotional Triggers: How to Spot and Manage Them

Everyone has emotional triggers—specific situations, words, or actions that spark intense emotional reactions. Identifying your emotional triggers allows you to gain more control over your emotional responses, reducing impulsive reactions and improving your relationships.

Jane and the Critical Feedback
Let's consider Jane, who always felt on edge when receiving critical feedback at work. Whenever her boss gave her constructive criticism, she would immediately become defensive and try to justify her actions without considering t,

feeling as if she was being attacked. One day, after another tense meeting, Jane sat down and reflected on her reaction. She realized her emotional trigger was rooted in her childhood, where any criticism felt like a personal attack. Once she identified this trigger, she was able to separate her past experience from the current situation and see feedback as an opportunity to improve rather than a judgment on her self-worth.

How to Identify Emotional Triggers:

- **Reflect on Past Reactions**: Think about moments where your emotions overwhelmed you. What was the situation, and what did someone say or do that triggered your response?

  Example: If you find yourself frustrated every time someone interrupts you, the trigger may stem from feeling disrespected or ignored.

- **Pay Attention to Your Body**: Emotions often manifest physically. A racing heart, clenched jaw, or tight chest can signal that you're being emotionally triggered. Use these sensations as early warning signs.

  Example: A racing heart during a conversation may indicate you're feeling anxious or defensive. Recognizing this allows you to pause and regroup before reacting impulsively.

- **Ask Why**: When you notice a strong emotional reaction, pause and ask yourself why. Are you responding to the situation at hand, or is it tied to something deeper?

  Example: Feeling rejected after a colleague doesn't respond to an idea could be tied to past experiences of not feeling heard.

The Five Components of Emotional Intelligence

Now that we've explored self-awareness and emotional triggers, let's dive deeper into the five key components of emotional intelligence and how they influence every aspect of our lives.

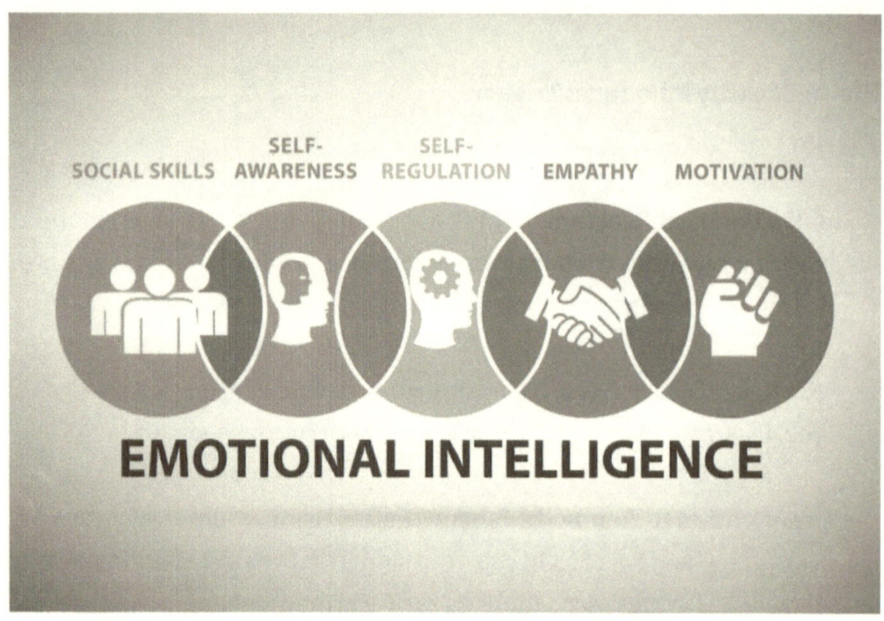

The five components

1) Self-Awareness

Self-awareness is about knowing what emotions you're feeling and why you're feeling them. The more self-aware you are, the better you can control your reactions and make intentional decisions.

Example: A frustrated project manager might pause and realize that the frustration stems from feeling unsupported. By acknowledging this, they can communicate their needs to their team rather than lashing out.

2) Self-Regulation

Self-regulation is the ability to manage your emotions and impulses. It's about choosing how to respond rather than reacting impulsively. People who practice self-regulation think before they act and are less likely to be controlled by their emotions.

Story: Mark, a teacher, once struggled with keeping calm when students acted out. He would often raise his voice in frustration. But once Mark learned self-regulation techniques—like pausing before reacting and taking deep breaths—he found that he could handle disruptive situations calmly, creating a more positive classroom environment.

3) Motivation

Motivation, in the context of EQ, means being driven by internal goals and personal growth rather than external rewards. Those with high emotional intelligence are motivated to learn, grow, and overcome challenges.

Example: A salesperson who stays motivated even after a tough week of rejections focuses on their long-term goals rather than immediate setbacks. Their drive comes from a desire to improve and succeed, not just to earn a bonus.

4) Empathy

Empathy allows you to connect with others on a deeper level by understanding and sharing their emotions. It's an essential skill for building strong relationships and fostering trust.

Story: Lisa, a team leader, used empathy to support a colleague going through a personal crisis. Instead of pushing them to keep up with deadlines, she listened, offered support, and adjusted their workload. This act of empathy not only improved their working relationship but also increased trust within the team.

5) Social Skills

People with high emotional intelligence are often excellent communicators and collaborators. They can navigate social complexities, manage conflict, and lead with empathy. These social skills help in creating environments of trust and cooperation.

Example: A manager who can skillfully navigate a conflict between two team members by understanding their perspectives and guiding them toward a resolution demonstrates strong EQ social skills.

Emotional intelligence is more than just understanding your feelings; it's about using that understanding to improve your relationships, decisions, and overall well-being. By recognizing your emotions and managing your reactions, you take the first step toward emotional mastery.

Before moving to the next chapter, take some time to reflect on your emotional triggers and your current level of self-awareness. Begin practicing the Emotional Check-In and start observing how your emotions influence your behavior. In the next chapter, we'll explore strategies for self-regulation—how to manage those intense emotions in challenging situations and respond calmly and effectively.

Chapter 2: Managing Your Emotions in Challenging Situations

Strategies for Self-Regulation

When Emotions Run High

Picture this: You're in the middle of a tense work meeting. You've prepared your presentation meticulously, yet halfway through, a senior colleague interrupts to point out flaws in your plan. A rush of heat rises to your face, frustration bubbles inside you. You want to snap back, defend yourself, maybe even throw in a snide comment to save face. But what if, instead of reacting on impulse, you paused, took a breath, and responded thoughtfully?

In these moments, self-regulation becomes your superpower. This isn't about bottling up emotions or suppressing how you feel—it's about channeling that emotional energy into more productive and empowering responses. It's the ability to steer the ship, even when the storm is raging inside.

The Science Behind Emotional Regulation: Why We React the Way We Do

Before diving into techniques, let's understand why our emotions sometimes take the wheel. Neuroscience shows that when we're triggered emotionally, the amygdala—our brain's "emotional alarm"—hijacks our response system. This "amygdala hijack" is what makes you want to yell at your partner during an argument or send that angry email you'll later regret. The brain's survival instincts kick in, preparing us to fight or flee. It's a primitive response that served our ancestors well when faced with physical danger but often backfires in today's social or professional situations.

This is where self-regulation comes into play. By engaging the prefrontal cortex—the part of the brain responsible for rational thinking and decision-making—you can override the emotional hijack and respond with intention rather than reflex.

1. Mindfulness: The Art of Noticing Before Reacting

Have you ever had one of those days where things just don't seem to go right? Maybe your alarm didn't go off, you spilled coffee on your shirt, and now you're running late for an important meeting. By the time you sit down, your mind is racing and your emotions are all over the place. In situations like these, mindfulness can be a game-changer.

Tim and the Mindful Pause

Tim, an ambitious young architect, had a hard time managing stress. Whenever deadlines loomed, he'd snap at his team and spiral into panic mode. One day, his mentor suggested he try mindfulness. Though skeptical at first, Tim gave it a shot. He started with just two minutes of mindful breathing before starting his day—nothing fancy, just sitting still and focusing on his breath. Over time, something remarkable happened: Tim found that he could handle stress much better. When things went wrong, instead of reacting impulsively, he was able to pause, take stock of his emotions, and choose his response. This simple practice of noticing his emotions before they took control transformed his work life.

Mindfulness Tip: It doesn't take a meditation retreat to start practicing mindfulness. Begin with just 30 seconds when you feel your emotions building up. Notice how your body feels, where the tension is, and what thoughts are running through your mind. Acknowledge those feelings without judgment.

This creates a space between the emotion and the action, allowing you to respond rather than react.

2. Cognitive Reframing: Turning Obstacles into Opportunities

Imagine getting harsh feedback from a boss. Instantly, your mind spirals: "I'm terrible at my job, I'll never be good enough." But what if you could take that same feedback and view it differently?

Nina's Transformation Through Reframing

Nina, a project manager, was crushed when her boss criticized her presentation style in front of her entire team. Her initial reaction was embarrassment and anger. She felt like she was being singled out, and it took everything in her not to fire back defensively. Later, while venting to a friend, Nina was encouraged to try cognitive reframing. Instead of viewing the feedback as a personal attack, what if she saw it as an opportunity to improve a skill? Nina sat down with this idea and worked through her feelings. The next time she received feedback, she approached it as a learning moment rather than a critique of her worth. Slowly, Nina began to thrive, using feedback as a tool for growth rather than a source of frustration.

Reframing in Action: The next time you face a difficult situation, ask yourself:

- What is another way to look at this?
- Is there a silver lining or lesson in this?
- How can I grow from this experience?

Shifting your perspective allows you to reduce the emotional charge of negative events and approach them with a problem-solving mindset.

3. The Grounding Technique: Pulling Yourself Back from Emotional Overload

Have you ever been so consumed by emotion that you felt completely ungrounded? Maybe you've experienced that panicky sensation where your thoughts race a mile a minute, and you can't seem to catch your breath. In moments like these, grounding techniques can be incredibly helpful to bring you back into the present.

Amy's Anxiety and Grounding Techniques

Amy, a lawyer juggling high-stakes cases, often found herself paralyzed by anxiety. She'd wake up in the middle of the night with her mind racing, unable to shake off the fear of failing her clients. One day, her therapist introduced her to grounding techniques. Whenever Amy felt anxiety creeping in, she'd focus on something physical—the texture of her desk, the sensation of her feet on the ground, or the weight of her hands resting on her lap. By tuning into her physical senses, Amy found that she could pull herself back from the brink of emotional overwhelm and regain her focus.

Try This Grounding Exercise: When emotions run high, try the 5-4-3-2-1 technique:

- Name **5 things** you can see.
- Name **4 things** you can touch.
- Name **3 things** you can hear.
- Name **2 things** you can smell.
- Name **1 thing** you can taste.

This simple exercise brings you back to the present moment and helps you regain control over your emotions.

4. The Power of the Pause: Taking Control of Your Reactions

It sounds almost too simple, but one of the most effective tools for emotional regulation is the pause. How many times have you said or done something in the heat of the moment, only to regret it later? If you can learn to pause, even for just a few seconds, you create space to choose your response rather than being swept away by emotion.

Jake's Temper and the Art of Pausing

Jake, a software engineer, had a short temper. His outbursts at work were well-known, and although he was brilliant at his job, his colleagues often kept their distance. After one particularly bad blow-up, Jake's manager suggested he take an anger management course. It was there that Jake learned the power of the pause. The next time he felt anger rising, instead of reacting immediately, Jake took a deep breath and counted to five. Those few seconds gave him the clarity to recognize that his anger wasn't really about the situation at hand—it was about feeling undervalued. With that insight, Jake was able to express his feelings calmly and productively.

Practice the Pause: The next time you feel a surge of emotion, commit to pausing for just three seconds before reacting. In that brief window, ask yourself:

- What am I really feeling right now?
- Is my reaction going to help or hurt the situation?
- What is the best response to align with my long-term goals?

That simple pause can change the trajectory of your response.

5. Building Long-Term Emotional Resilience: The Role of Healthy Habits

Self-regulation is not just about managing emotions in the heat of the moment. It's also about building long-term emotional resilience through healthy habits. How you treat your body and mind on a daily basis has a profound impact on your emotional well-being.

Carla's Journey to Emotional Resilience

Carla, a corporate executive, was known for her high-stress lifestyle. Late nights, skipped meals, and no exercise left her constantly on edge. Her breaking point came when she burst into tears during a board meeting—a situation that left her feeling humiliated. Realizing she needed to make a change, Carla started small. She began waking up 30 minutes earlier to go for a run and set a strict rule of no emails after 8 p.m. She also started journaling each night, reflecting on her emotions. Over time, Carla noticed a profound shift. She felt calmer, more in control, and better equipped to handle the inevitable stresses of her job.

Healthy Habits to Boost Self-Regulation:

- **Exercise**: Physical activity releases endorphins that improve mood and reduce stress.
- **Sleep**: Aim for 7-9 hours of sleep to recharge your brain and improve emotional control.
- **Nutrition**: Eating a balanced diet rich in fruits, vegetables, and whole grains supports cognitive function and emotional health.
- **Journaling**: Writing about your emotions can help you process and regulate your feelings, making you less likely to be overwhelmed by them.

Becoming the Captain of Your Emotional Ship

Emotional regulation isn't about being perfect or never getting upset—it's about learning to steer your emotions in a direction that serves you, even in challenging situations. By integrating mindfulness, reframing, grounding, pausing, and healthy habits, you'll cultivate the resilience to navigate life's storms with grace and confidence.

Chapter 3: Cultivating Empathy in Everyday Life

Understanding and Sharing the Feelings of Others

The Heart of Connection

Think about a time when you felt utterly alone in a crowd—when you were surrounded by people but felt no one truly understood what you were going through. Maybe it was during a personal crisis or a stressful work situation. Empathy is about bridging that gap of isolation and genuinely connecting with others on an emotional level. It's not just about offering words of comfort; it's about creating a space where people feel truly seen and heard.

Empathy has the power to transform interactions and build meaningful relationships. It's a crucial skill that can enhance your personal connections and improve your professional life. Let's explore how cultivating empathy can address common pain points and create a more supportive environment for everyone.

The Essence of Empathy: What It Really Means

Empathy goes beyond surface-level sympathy. It involves truly understanding and experiencing the emotions of others. When we're empathetic, we connect with people on a deeper level, providing comfort and validation.

Emily's Dilemma

Emily, a single mother juggling multiple jobs, often felt overwhelmed and isolated. One day, she confided in her coworker, Jack, about her struggles with balancing work and parenting. Instead of offering generic advice or a superficial response, Jack shared his own experiences with burnout and exhaustion. He related to her struggles and offered her his support, like helping with tasks at work to ease her load and giving her time to breathe. Emily felt seen for the first time and appreciated Jack's genuine empathy, which strengthened their bond and made her feel less alone.

The Benefits of Empathy: Building Stronger Relationships

Empathy isn't just a feel-good concept; it has tangible benefits:

- **Enhanced Relationships**: When people feel understood, they are more likely to open up and build stronger connections.
- **Improved Communication**: Empathy fosters effective communication by addressing underlying emotions and needs.
- **Conflict Resolution**: Understanding others' perspectives can help resolve conflicts more constructively.

Sarah's Leadership Transformation

Sarah, a project manager, struggled with team conflicts and low morale. By adopting an empathetic approach, she began to actively listen to her team members' concerns and frustrations. For instance, she noticed that team member Alex was frequently quiet during meetings. Instead of assuming disinterest and charging him, Sarah took the time to understand that Alex felt overshadowed by more vocal colleagues. By addressing this issue and encouraging Alex to share his ideas, Sarah improved team cohesion and performance.

1. Active Listening: The Foundation of Empathy

Active listening is the cornerstone of empathy. It involves fully engaging with the speaker and showing that you are genuinely interested in their experience.

Story: Mark's Listening Challenge

Mark, a busy executive, often found himself distracted during conversations with his employees. He realized this was affecting his relationships and team dynamics. To improve, Mark made a conscious effort to practice active listening. He started setting aside dedicated time for one-on-one meetings, during which he would put away his phone and computer, maintaining eye contact and nodding in understanding. His employees began to open up more, sharing valuable insights and concerns that had previously gone unnoticed. Mark's engagement led to a more collaborative and effective work environment.

How to Practice Active Listening:

- **Give Full Attention**: Eliminate distractions and focus entirely on the speaker.
- **Reflect and Paraphrase**: Summarize what the speaker has said to show understanding and validate their feelings.
- **Ask Open-Ended Questions**: Encourage further discussion and exploration of their thoughts and feelings.

2. Empathic Reflection: Putting Yourself in Their Shoes

Empathic reflection involves not just understanding but also communicating that understanding to the other person. It's about reflecting back their emotions to validate their experience.

Story: Lisa's Empathic Approach

Lisa, a nurse, encountered a patient named Joan who was struggling with a recent diagnosis. Joan felt scared and alone, expressing her fears in a way that felt overwhelming. Instead of offering generic reassurances, Lisa practiced empathic reflection. She acknowledged Joan's fear by saying, "It sounds like you're feeling really overwhelmed and uncertain about what's next." This validation helped Joan feel heard and supported, leading to a more trusting relationship with Lisa and a better overall patient experience.

How to Use Empathic Reflection:

- **Acknowledge Feelings**: Use statements like, "I understand that you're feeling..." to show that you recognize their emotions.
- **Validate Emotions**: Reinforce that their feelings are legitimate and important.
- **Provide Support**: Offer specific assistance or reassurance based on their needs.

3. Developing Emotional Awareness: Tune Into Others' Feelings

Emotional awareness involves recognizing and interpreting the emotions of others through both verbal and non-verbal cues. It requires a keen sense of observation and sensitivity.

Story: David's Insight

David, a high school principal, noticed that his staff was becoming increasingly disengaged and stressed. Instead of attributing this to a lack of motivation, he decided to pay closer attention to their interactions and body language. He observed signs of burnout and frustration during meetings and started initiating private check-ins with staff members. By addressing their concerns and offering support, David was able to address issues before they escalated and improve overall staff morale.

Tips for Developing Emotional Awareness:

- **Observe Non-Verbal Cues**: Pay attention to body language, facial expressions, and tone of voice.

- **Tune Into Emotions**: Notice how others' emotions impact their behavior and communication.
- **Ask and Clarify**: If you're unsure about someone's feelings, ask open-ended questions to gain clarity.

4. Cultivating Empathy Through Perspective-Taking

Perspective-taking involves imagining yourself in someone else's situation and understanding their viewpoint. It's a powerful tool for empathy that helps bridge gaps in understanding.

Story: Anna's Perspective Shift

Anna, a customer service manager, had a particularly challenging customer who frequently complained about delays. Initially, Anna felt frustrated and impatient. However, she decided to try perspective-taking. She imagined herself in the customer's shoes—perhaps dealing with pressing deadlines and frustration. This shift in perspective allowed Anna to respond with greater patience and understanding, ultimately leading to a more positive resolution and a more satisfied customer.

How to Practice Perspective-Taking:

- **Imagine Their Experience**: Visualize what it would be like to be in their position.
- **Consider Their Context**: Think about external factors influencing their emotions and behavior.
- **Respond with Understanding**: Use your insights to guide your responses and interactions.

5. Building Empathy in Teams and Organizations

Creating a culture of empathy within teams and organizations involves fostering an environment where open communication, mutual respect, and support are prioritized. This leads to improved collaboration and a more positive work atmosphere.

Story: The Compassionate Company

A tech company faced high employee turnover and low engagement. The HR team decided to implement empathy-driven practices, including regular feedback sessions and empathy training workshops. They encouraged managers to practice active listening and provide emotional support to their teams. As a result, employee satisfaction and retention improved significantly, and the workplace became known for its supportive and empathetic culture.

Steps to Foster Empathy in the Workplace:

- **Encourage Open Communication**: Create opportunities for employees to share their thoughts and feelings.
- **Provide Training and Resources**: Offer workshops and tools to develop emotional intelligence and empathy skills.
- **Lead by Example**: Demonstrate empathetic behavior as a leader and encourage others to do the same.

The Ripple Effect of Empathy

Empathy is a transformative force that enhances personal and professional relationships. By practicing active listening, empathic reflection, emotional awareness, and perspective-taking, you foster deeper connections and create a more supportive environment.

Chapter 4: Mastering Social Skills for Stronger Connections

Communicate, Collaborate, and Build Lasting Relationships

The Key to Thriving in a Connected World

We live in an age where connections and networking are key to success, both personally and professionally. Whether you're leading a team at work, managing relationships with friends and family, or meeting new people, social skills play an essential role in your ability to thrive. Yet, how often have you found yourself feeling misunderstood, struggling to get your point across, or dealing with conflicts that seem impossible to resolve?

In this chapter, we will explore how to develop essential social skills that can help you navigate these challenges. From effective communication to conflict resolution and collaboration, mastering social skills is the foundation for building deeper, more meaningful connections.

The Power of Social Skills: Why They Matter

Research has consistently shown that people with strong social skills are more successful in both their personal and professional lives. According to a study published in *The Harvard Business Review*, employees with high emotional intelligence, including strong social skills, tend to outperform their peers by a significant margin, earning higher salaries and advancing faster in their careers .

Social skills are not just about being charming or outgoing—they involve a range of abilities such as listening, empathy, clear communication, and problem-solving. These skills allow us to build trust, foster collaboration, and create a positive environment around us.

> *"Success in life is founded upon attention to the small things. Many of us fail to succeed because we're not aware of the little things that build or destroy trust."* — *Dale Carnegie,* How to Win Friends and Influence People

1. Effective Communication: The Art of Being Understood

Effective communication is about much more than just talking; it's about ensuring that your message is understood and received in the way you intend. This involves clarity, active listening, and emotional intelligence.

Sarah's Communication Breakthrough

Sarah, a product manager, struggled to communicate her ideas clearly in meetings. She often found that her team misunderstood her suggestions, leading to delays and frustration. One day, she decided to apply an exercise in **concise communication**. She began structuring her points into a simple formula: "What, Why, and How." For example, instead of saying, "We need to change our marketing approach," she would say, "We need to shift our marketing approach (What), because the current strategy isn't reaching our target audience (Why). Here's how we can improve it (How)." This clarity improved team collaboration and led to more efficient decision-making.

A study published in the *Journal of Personality and Social Psychology* found that **clarity in communication** significantly improves workplace productivity and reduces conflict. Clear, concise communication helps ensure that everyone is on the same page, minimizing misunderstandings and fostering a more collaborative environment.

Exercise: The Clear Communication Challenge

Try this exercise in your next meeting or conversation:

- **Step 1**: Before speaking, take a moment to organize your thoughts.
-
- **Step 2**: Use the "What, Why, How" method to structure your message.
-
- **Step 3**: After you've spoken, ask the listener to paraphrase what they heard to ensure clarity.

2. Conflict Resolution: Navigating Difficult Conversations

Conflicts are inevitable in any relationship, whether personal or professional. However, how you handle them can make all the difference. The key to resolving conflicts lies in approaching the situation with empathy, active listening, and problem-solving skills.

Story: David and Maria's Conflict at Work

David and Maria worked together on a marketing team but often found themselves butting heads. Their arguments started over small things, like how to format reports, but soon escalated to larger issues about strategy. Instead of avoiding each other, they decided to apply the **Conflict Resolution Model**. First, they agreed to listen to each other's concerns without interrupting. David realized that Maria's insistence on certain formats came from a desire for clarity, while Maria learned that David valued flexibility in approach. By focusing on the underlying needs behind their positions, they found a compromise that worked for both of them.

According to psychologist Daniel Goleman, who popularized the concept of emotional intelligence, **emotional self-regulation** is crucial in conflict resolution. He notes that people who can manage their emotions during conflict are more likely to reach peaceful resolutions .

Exercise: Conflict Resolution Role-Play

- **Step 1**: Identify a recent conflict you've experienced.
- **Step 2**: Imagine how you could have handled it differently using empathy and active listening.
- **Step 3**: If possible, role-play the situation with a friend or colleague to practice this new approach.

3. Building Trust: The Foundation of Social Skills

Trust is the cornerstone of any meaningful relationship. Without trust, communication falters, collaboration becomes difficult, and conflicts arise more frequently. But building trust requires consistency, transparency, and vulnerability.

John's Trust-Building Journey

John, a sales executive, struggled to build trust with his clients. He was skilled in making initial sales pitches but often found that his clients hesitated to work with him long-term. After reflecting on his approach, he realized that he wasn't showing enough vulnerability or transparency. Instead of always trying to appear perfect, he started being more open about the challenges his company faced and how they were working to overcome them. By doing so, he built stronger, more lasting relationships with his clients.

A study conducted by researchers at the University of California found that **vulnerability**—the willingness to admit mistakes or ask for help—plays a key role in building trust . When people feel that you are authentic and transparent, they are more likely to trust and engage with you.

Exercise: Trust-Building with Vulnerability

- **Step 1**: In your next interaction, share something personal or admit a mistake, even if it feels uncomfortable.
- **Step 2**: Observe how the other person responds.
- **Step 3**: Continue to practice vulnerability to strengthen trust over time.

4. Collaboration: Working Together Effectively

Collaboration is about more than just working alongside others—it's about blending diverse perspectives, skills, and ideas to achieve a common goal. Effective collaboration requires both emotional intelligence and strong communication.

The Struggling Team

A startup team faced major setbacks when its members couldn't align on key project decisions. Frustration grew, and team productivity plummeted. Their CEO stepped in and introduced **collaborative problem-solving** exercises. They were asked to share their individual concerns openly and propose solutions without judgment. This approach allowed them to understand each other's perspectives better, build trust, and eventually work together more effectively, resulting in a breakthrough on their project.

A study in the *Journal of Applied Psychology* found that teams with higher levels of emotional intelligence demonstrated significantly better performance, especially in high-stress environments . Emotional intelligence fosters a collaborative spirit and enhances team dynamics.

Exercise: Collaborative Brainstorming

- **Step 1**: In your next team meeting, introduce a problem that needs to be solved.
- **Step 2**: Ask each team member to share their thoughts and solutions

without interruption or judgment.

- **Step 3**: Combine ideas to create a collaborative solution that incorporates everyone's input.

5. Social Awareness: Reading the Room

Social awareness is the ability to pick up on the emotions, motivations, and dynamics of the people around you. This skill is essential for adapting your behavior to different social contexts and creating positive interactions.

Emma's Misstep

Emma, a junior manager, was excited about presenting her new ideas during a department meeting. However, she failed to notice that her team had just received negative feedback from the senior leadership, leaving them frustrated and distracted. By ignoring the emotional tone of the room, Emma's presentation fell flat, and her ideas were met with resistance. Emma later reflected on how she could have adapted her approach by first addressing the team's concerns and then introducing her ideas in a more empathetic way.

Research published in *Psychological Science* found that individuals who are more attuned to the emotional states of others tend to be more successful in both social and professional settings . Social awareness helps in navigating complex interactions and ensures more positive outcomes.

Exercise: Practice Reading Social Cues

- **Step 1**: During your next group interaction, focus on observing non-verbal cues like body language, tone of voice, and facial expressions.
- **Step 2**: Try to gauge the emotional atmosphere in the room.
- **Step 3**: Adapt your approach based on the mood and energy of the group.

Social Skills as a Gateway to Success

Mastering social skills isn't just about becoming more likable—it's about building genuine connections, fostering trust, and creating an environment where everyone can thrive. Whether it's through effective communication, conflict resolution, trust-building, or collaboration, these skills will elevate your relationships and help you navigate life's challenges with ease.

Choose one social skill you'd like to improve—whether it's active listening, building trust, or conflict resolution—and put it into practice this week. By consistently working on these skills, you'll create deeper, more meaningful connections in both your personal and professional life.

Chapter 5: Managing Relationships for Long-Term Success

Fostering Strong Connections at Home, Work, and Beyond

The Lifeblood of Emotional Intelligence

In our fast-paced, digital world, the quality of our relationships often determines the quality of our lives. Whether at home, at work, or within our social circles, managing relationships effectively is essential for long-term happiness and success. However, it's not always easy—misunderstandings, unmet expectations, and unresolved conflicts can strain even the strongest bonds.

This chapter will help you learn how emotional intelligence (EQ) plays a pivotal role in navigating the complexities of relationships. Drawing on research, real-life stories, and actionable exercises, you'll discover how to deepen your connections, strengthen trust, resolve conflicts with empathy, and maintain emotional balance.

Relationship Awareness: Understanding the Dynamics of Connection

At the heart of any relationship lies an understanding of its unique dynamics—whether it's a relationship with a spouse, a colleague, or a friend. Emotional intelligence helps us recognize these dynamics by providing the insight to read emotions, needs, and expectations accurately.

John's Workplace Revelation

John was a talented software developer who struggled with collaboration. Despite being brilliant technically, he couldn't connect well with his teammates, which led to tension. His team often felt John was dismissive, while John believed his colleagues were slowing him down. During a team-building workshop, John realized that his failure to pick up on social cues was alienating his coworkers. He started practicing **relationship awareness**, actively paying attention to his colleagues' emotional responses, and asking more questions to understand their perspectives. Over time, he developed deeper connections and fostered a more supportive work environment.

The Value of Social Capital

Social capital refers to the networks and relationships that enable society to function effectively. According to research from the OECD (Organisation for Economic Co-operation and Development), individuals with strong social capital—meaning those with robust relationships—experience higher life satisfaction, better mental health, and greater professional success. This highlights how **relationship awareness** enhances both our personal well-being and professional productivity.

Enhancing Relationship Awareness

This exercise will help you identify the emotional dynamics in your relationships and take action to improve them:

- **Step 1**: Identify five key relationships in your life (e.g., partner, friend, coworker).
- **Step 2**: Reflect on each relationship's current state. Are there any recurring misunderstandings or emotional patterns?
- **Step 3**: Ask yourself: How might the other person perceive the relationship? What emotional needs might they have that I haven't addressed?

- **Step 4**: For each relationship, schedule a conversation where you actively listen to the other person's thoughts and feelings. Focus on validating their emotions without immediately reacting or trying to fix the issue.
- **Step 5**: Reflect on how this exercise changes the dynamics of the relationship over time. Journaling your findings can help identify patterns and improvements.

Managing Conflict: From Tension to Resolution

Conflict is inevitable in relationships, but it doesn't have to be destructive. In fact, if handled correctly, conflict can deepen trust and lead to growth. Emotionally intelligent individuals approach conflict with empathy and a genuine desire to resolve the issue rather than win the argument.

Lisa and Tom's Marital Conflict

Lisa and Tom had been arguing for weeks about household responsibilities. Both were frustrated and felt their efforts were underappreciated. After reading about emotional intelligence, Lisa decided to try a new approach. Instead of accusing Tom of not doing enough, she expressed her feelings using **nonviolent communication** (NVC). "I feel overwhelmed when the dishes pile up after dinner," she said. This non-judgmental statement opened a dialogue rather than sparking another argument. Tom admitted he had no idea how much stress it caused her and agreed to share the load. Together, they worked out a more balanced schedule, strengthening their bond in the process.

Constructive Conflict

According to research published in the *Journal of Organizational Behavior*, conflicts that are handled constructively lead to better decision-making, increased creativity, and stronger relationships. In contrast, unresolved or poorly managed conflict increases stress and can lead to resentment, disconnection, and even health problems .

Additional Exercise: Conflict De-escalation Techniques

The next time you're faced with a conflict, practice these three de-escalation techniques:

- **Step 1**: Take a pause before reacting. Deep breaths activate your parasympathetic nervous system, which helps you calm down before responding.
- **Step 2**: Use "I" statements to express how you feel without blaming the other person (e.g., "I feel stressed when deadlines are tight" vs. "You never meet deadlines").
- **Step 3**: Repeat back what the other person has said to show you're listening. This validates their perspective, even if you don't agree.
- Example: "I hear you're upset because you feel I've been distant lately."

Bonus Tip: After resolving a conflict, check back in with the person later. A simple "How are you feeling about our conversation?" can strengthen trust and keep communication open.

Building Trust: The Foundation of Lasting Relationships

Trust is often described as the currency of relationships—once it's broken, it can be difficult to rebuild. But trust doesn't just magically appear; it requires time, consistency, and vulnerability. Emotionally intelligent people understand that trust must be nurtured through actions, words, and presence.

Rebuilding Trust in a Business Partnership

Mike and Steve, co-founders of a tech startup, hit a major roadblock when they disagreed about the direction of their company. Their heated arguments started to damage their professional relationship. After a few rocky months, they decided to work with a business coach who emphasized **trust-building through transparency**. They made a commitment to communicate openly and regularly, even about difficult topics. By holding each other accountable and being vulnerable about their fears and concerns, they gradually rebuilt their trust, and their business flourished as a result.

Trust and Oxytocin

Neuroscientific research has shown that the hormone **oxytocin** is linked to feelings of trust and bonding. When people experience emotional closeness—whether through touch, eye contact, or shared vulnerability—oxytocin levels rise, fostering deeper connection. However, trust can be eroded through inconsistent behavior, secrecy, or lack of empathy, which triggers stress hormones like cortisol. In the workplace, studies show that employees in high-trust organizations report 74% less stress, 106% more energy, and 50% higher productivity .

Additional Exercise: The Trust Inventory

This exercise will help you build (or rebuild) trust in key relationships:

- **Step 1**: Think of a person with whom you'd like to strengthen trust.
- **Step 2**: Reflect on your past interactions with this person. Are there any actions or behaviors that may have eroded trust?
- **Step 3**: Identify two to three specific actions you can take to demonstrate reliability, honesty, or vulnerability with this person.
- **Step 4**: Monitor your interactions over the next few weeks. Do you notice any shifts in the relationship?
- **Step 5**: Follow up with the person, asking them how they feel about the trust level in your relationship.

Emotional Support: The Glue that Holds Relationships Together

Emotional support is the willingness to be there for someone during times of need—whether by providing a listening ear, offering words of encouragement, or simply being present. It's one of the most vital components of any healthy relationship, but it's often overlooked when life gets busy.

Story: Rachel's Friendship Breakthrough

Rachel had been drifting apart from her best friend Megan, who was going through a rough time. Megan had just lost her job, and Rachel, caught up in her own hectic life, didn't realize how much support her friend needed. One afternoon, Rachel received a text from Megan: "I feel like I'm losing everything." Rachel realized she had been distant and immediately called Megan, simply to listen. Instead of offering advice, Rachel let Megan share her frustrations and pain. That act of emotional support not only strengthened their bond but reminded Rachel of the power of presence.

Emotional Support and Longevity

A study published in *Psychosomatic Medicine* found that emotional support not only reduces stress but also has long-term physical health benefits. Individuals who receive emotional support from close relationships are more likely to recover from illness, cope with major life changes, and live longer . Emotional support fosters resilience and provides a buffer against stress-related health problems.

Additional Exercise: The Emotional Support Audit

To become more mindful of how you offer and receive emotional support, try this exercise:

- **Step 1**: Think of two people in your life who might benefit from emotional support.
- **Step 2**: Reach out to each of them, asking, "How can I support you right now?"
- **Step 3**: Offer support based on their response, whether it's listening, helping with a task, or simply spending time with them.
- **Step 4**: Reflect on how offering emotional support impacts both your well-being and your relationship.

Bonus Tip: Remember, emotional support goes both ways. It's equally important to **ask for support** when you need it. Don't be afraid to lean on others during tough times—it strengthens relationships and creates a balanced exchange.

Maintaining Balance: Avoiding Burnout in Relationships

Investing in relationships is rewarding, but it's crucial to maintain a healthy balance. Emotional intelligence allows us to set boundaries and manage expectations without feeling guilty. When we stretch ourselves too thin, burnout can occur, leading to resentment and relationship strain.

Sara's Boundary Dilemma

Sara was always the go-to person for her friends and family. Whether it was helping someone move, offering advice, or lending money, she never said no. Eventually, Sara started to feel overwhelmed and drained but didn't know how to step back without hurting her loved ones. After attending a workshop on emotional intelligence, she realized the importance of setting boundaries to avoid burnout. Sara began by politely declining some requests for help and explaining her need for downtime. Surprisingly, her friends respected her decisions and appreciated her honesty.

Compassion Fatigue and Boundary Setting

Studies have shown that **compassion fatigue**—a state of emotional exhaustion from over-giving—can lead to anxiety, depression, and health issues. A 2020 report by the American Psychological Association suggests that caregivers and highly empathetic individuals are at particular risk for burnout. The solution? **Setting boundaries** and practicing self-care. These strategies allow individuals to maintain long-term relationships without sacrificing their own well-being.

Additional Exercise: The Boundary-Setting Checklist

If you struggle with setting boundaries, this exercise will help you take practical steps:

- **Step 1**: Identify areas in your life where you feel overextended (e.g., at work, with friends, in your family).
- **Step 2**: Consider what you need to feel emotionally balanced (e.g., more time for yourself, less commitment to certain activities).
- **Step 3**: Practice communicating your boundaries with kindness and clarity (e.g., "I would love to help, but I need some time to recharge this weekend").
- **Step 4**: Monitor how setting boundaries improves your energy, mood, and relationships.

The Lifelong Process of Relationship Management

Managing relationships requires constant attention, emotional intelligence, and a willingness to grow. Whether you're navigating personal bonds or professional connections, focusing on trust, emotional support, conflict resolution, and balance can lead to stronger, healthier relationships that stand the test of time.

Think about your everyday relationships and choose one relationship where you'd like to see improvement. Apply one principle from this chapter—whether it's offering emotional support, setting a boundary, or practicing conflict resolution—and observe how the relationship evolves. Remember, small, consistent changes can lead to profound long-term improvements.

Chapter 6: Emotional Intelligence at Work

The Power of Emotional Intelligence in the Workplace

Emotional Intelligence (EI) is a cornerstone of career success. Studies show that professionals with high EI are more likely to excel in their roles, build strong teams, and advance in their careers. According to a 2019 report by TalentSmart, EI accounts for 58% of job performance across various industries. Additionally, Harvard Business Review highlights that leaders with high emotional intelligence can significantly influence organizational culture and drive performance.

Understanding Workplace Emotional Dynamics

Imagine a manager named Alex, known for his exceptional leadership skills. Alex's team faced a challenging project with tight deadlines. Instead of solely focusing on the technical aspects, Alex paid attention to his team's emotional needs. He held regular check-ins to gauge their stress levels, offered support, and acknowledged their efforts. As a result, his team remained motivated and performed exceptionally well, leading to the project's success.

Alex's story illustrates how understanding and addressing emotional dynamics can lead to a more engaged and productive team. Recognizing emotions in yourself and others, and responding effectively, is key to fostering a positive work environment.

Building Strong Relationships Through Emotional Intelligence

A study published in the Journal of Applied Psychology found that teams with higher emotional intelligence exhibit better communication, collaboration, and problem-solving skills. These teams are also more adaptable to change and less prone to conflict.

Exercise: The Emotional Intelligence Inventory

To build strong workplace relationships, start with an Emotional Intelligence Inventory:

- **Step 1**: List your key workplace relationships—colleagues, supervisors, subordinates.
- **Step 2**: For each relationship, evaluate how well you understand and respond to their emotional needs. Consider factors such as empathy, communication style, and conflict resolution.
- **Step 3**: Identify areas for improvement and develop strategies to enhance these relationships. For example, if you struggle with empathy, commit to practicing active listening and validation.

The Takeaway

Understanding and improving your emotional dynamics with colleagues can lead to more effective teamwork and stronger professional connections.

Managing Conflicts with Emotional Intelligence

Consider the case of Jane, a team leader who faced a conflict between two team members, Tom and Lisa. Rather than taking sides or ignoring the issue, Jane facilitated a meeting where both parties could express their concerns and feelings. She used active listening techniques to ensure each person felt heard and valued. By addressing the underlying emotions and finding common ground, Jane helped Tom and Lisa resolve their conflict and improve their working relationship.

This story exemplifies how using emotional intelligence to manage conflicts can lead to more effective resolutions and foster a more collaborative work environment.

Exercise: The Conflict Resolution Role-Play

To practice conflict management, engage in a role-play exercise:

- **Step 1**: Identify a common workplace conflict scenario (e.g., differing opinions on a project).
- **Step 2**: Partner with a colleague to role-play both sides of the conflict.
- **Step 3**: Focus on using emotional intelligence skills such as empathy, active listening, and effective communication to resolve the issue.
- **Step 4**: Debrief after the role-play to discuss what strategies worked and what could be improved.

The Takeaway

Practicing conflict resolution skills through role-play helps you handle real-world disputes more effectively, enhancing your professional relationships and team dynamics.

Leveraging Emotional Intelligence for Career Advancement

A study by the Center for Creative Leadership found that emotional intelligence is a key predictor of leadership success. Leaders with high EI are better at managing stress, motivating their teams, and navigating organizational politics. This ability to handle complex emotional landscapes can set you apart as a candidate for promotion and leadership roles.

The Career Climber

Laura, a mid-level manager, used her emotional intelligence to advance her career. She proactively sought feedback, managed her stress effectively, and demonstrated empathy towards her team. By applying these skills, Laura was recognized for her leadership abilities and promoted to a senior management position.

Exercise: The Career Reflection Exercise

To leverage EQ for career advancement:

- **Step 1**: Reflect on your career goals and how emotional intelligence can help you achieve them.
- **Step 2**: Identify key EI skills that are relevant to your career aspirations (e.g., emotional regulation for high-pressure roles, empathy for leadership positions).
- **Step 3**: Develop a plan to enhance these skills through training, feedback, and practice.
- **Step 4**: Set specific, measurable goals for applying EI in your current role and track your progress.

The Takeaway

Applying emotional intelligence skills strategically can help you advance in your career by improving your leadership capabilities and overall job performance.

Creating a Positive Work Environment

In a company where employee morale was low, Sarah, an HR manager, decided to use emotional intelligence to transform the workplace culture. She initiated regular team-building activities, open feedback sessions, and recognition programs. By focusing on understanding and addressing employees' emotional needs, Sarah created a more positive and productive work environment. Employee satisfaction and performance improved significantly, demonstrating the impact of a supportive workplace culture.

Exercise: The Workplace Culture Assessment

To contribute to a positive work environment:

- **Step 1**: Assess the current emotional climate of your workplace. Consider factors such as employee satisfaction, communication effectiveness, and overall morale.

- **Step 2**: Identify areas where emotional intelligence could enhance the workplace culture (e.g., improving team communication, increasing recognition).
- **Step 3**: Develop and implement strategies to address these areas. This might include introducing regular feedback sessions or creating a peer recognition program.
- **Step 4**: Monitor the impact of these strategies and adjust your approach as needed.

The Takeaway

Enhancing the emotional climate of your workplace contributes to a more positive and productive environment, benefiting both employees and organizational performance.

Navigating Office Politics with Emotional Intelligence

Tom was a mid-level manager who found himself caught in office politics between competing departments. Instead of taking sides, he used his emotional intelligence to navigate the situation diplomatically. He built strong relationships with key stakeholders, listened actively to different perspectives, and sought common ground. By understanding the emotional drivers behind the political dynamics, Tom managed to foster collaboration and build alliances, ultimately positioning himself as a trusted leader within the organization.

Exercise: The Political Dynamics Map

To handle office politics:

- **Step 1**: Create a map of the key players and power dynamics in your workplace. Identify their roles, influence, and any existing alliances or conflicts.
- **Step 2**: Analyze each individual's emotional drivers and motivations.

Consider what matters to them and how they influence their actions.
- **Step 3**: Develop strategies to build positive relationships and navigate the political landscape effectively. Focus on finding common interests and creating win-win situations.

The Takeaway

Understanding and managing office politics through emotional intelligence can help you navigate complex professional environments and build influential relationships.

Enhancing Emotional Resilience in High-Stress Environments

A study published in the International Journal of Stress Management found that employees with high emotional intelligence are better equipped to manage stress and prevent burnout. These individuals are more adept at recognizing stressors, regulating their emotions, and employing coping strategies effectively.

The Resilient Consultant

Emily, a consultant working on high-stakes projects with tight deadlines, faced significant stress in her role. By applying emotional intelligence techniques, such as mindfulness and self-awareness, she managed to stay composed and focused. She also encouraged her team to adopt similar practices, fostering a resilient work environment where everyone could handle pressure more effectively.

Exercise: The Stress Resilience Toolkit

To enhance emotional resilience:

- **Step 1**: Identify your primary stressors at work and assess how they impact your emotional well-being.
- **Step 2**: Develop a toolkit of resilience strategies, such as mindfulness exercises, time management techniques, and relaxation practices.

- **Step 3**: Implement these strategies in your daily routine and monitor their effectiveness. Adjust your toolkit as needed based on what works best for you.

The Takeaway

Building emotional resilience through effective stress management techniques helps you maintain performance and well-being in high-pressure situations.

The Role of Emotional Intelligence in Innovation and Creativity

Research published in the Creativity Research Journal indicates that emotional intelligence is strongly linked to creative problem-solving and innovation. EI enhances your ability to approach problems from multiple perspectives and remain open to new ideas.

The Innovative Team Leader

David, a team leader at a tech company, encouraged a culture of creativity by leveraging emotional intelligence. He created an environment where team members felt safe to share unconventional ideas without fear of judgment. By fostering an emotionally supportive atmosphere, David's team developed several innovative solutions that significantly advanced their projects.

Exercise: The Creativity Enhancement Exercise

To boost creativity and innovation:

- **Step 1**: Identify a current challenge or project where you want to foster creativity.
- **Step 2**: Use brainstorming techniques, such as mind mapping or free writing, to generate a wide range of ideas.
- **Step 3**: Implement emotional intelligence skills by creating a supportive environment for idea sharing and constructive feedback.
- **Step 4**: Reflect on how the application of EI affects the creativity and

effectiveness of your solutions.

The Takeaway

Leveraging emotional intelligence to create a supportive and open environment enhances creativity and innovation, leading to more effective problem-solving.

Emotional Intelligence for Effective Networking

Maria, a business development executive, used her emotional intelligence to excel at networking events. She focused on building genuine connections rather than just exchanging business cards. By actively listening, showing empathy, and expressing authentic interest in others, Maria formed valuable relationships that led to successful business partnerships and career opportunities.

Exercise: The Networking Strategy Plan

To improve your networking skills:

- **Step 1**: Identify key networking events or opportunities relevant to your career goals.
- **Step 2**: Develop a strategy for building meaningful connections, including active listening, asking insightful questions, and following up after interactions.
- **Step 3**: Practice these skills in various networking scenarios and evaluate their effectiveness in forming valuable relationships.

The Takeaway

Applying emotional intelligence to networking helps you build more meaningful and productive professional relationships.

The Impact of Emotional Intelligence on Team Morale and Productivity

A study published in the Journal of Organizational Behavior found that teams with high emotional intelligence demonstrate higher levels of morale, collaboration, and overall productivity. EI contributes to a positive work environment, reducing turnover and increasing job satisfaction.

The Morale Booster

Lucas, a team leader at a marketing firm, noticed a decline in his team's morale. He took proactive steps to address the issue by organizing team-building activities, providing regular feedback, and recognizing individual contributions. By focusing on emotional intelligence, Lucas was able to boost team morale and enhance productivity, resulting in improved project outcomes.

Exercise: The Team Morale Assessment

To improve team morale:

- **Step 1**: Conduct a survey or feedback session to assess the current state of team morale and identify areas of concern.
- **Step 2**: Develop and implement strategies to address these concerns, such as team-building activities, recognition programs, or communication improvements.
- **Step 3**: Monitor the impact of these strategies on team morale and productivity, and make adjustments as needed.

The Takeaway

Enhancing team morale through emotional intelligence strategies leads to increased productivity and a more positive work environment.

Emotional intelligence is not just a personal asset but a professional necessity. By understanding and applying EI in the workplace, you can improve relationships, manage conflicts, advance your career, and contribute to a positive work environment. The skills and strategies outlined in this chapter will help you harness the power of emotional intelligence to achieve success and fulfillment in your professional life.

Conclusion: The Lifelong Journey of Emotional Intelligence

Emotional intelligence is not a destination, but a lifelong journey—a process of continuous learning, growth, and adaptation. As you've explored throughout this book, mastering emotional intelligence can transform every aspect of your life. From self-awareness and emotional regulation to empathy and relationship management, the skills you've developed empower you to navigate life's challenges with greater confidence, resilience, and understanding.

But perhaps the most important takeaway is this: emotional intelligence isn't about perfection. It's about progress. Life will continue to throw obstacles your way—difficult relationships, stressful situations, and emotional setbacks. However, the emotional intelligence toolkit you now possess will help you face these moments with grace and wisdom.

Why Emotional Intelligence Matters More Than Ever

In today's fast-paced world, where technology often distances us from genuine connection, emotional intelligence is a superpower. It's what bridges the gap between superficial interaction and meaningful connection, between reacting impulsively and responding thoughtfully. As we face a future filled with unpredictability—whether in our careers, personal lives, or society at large—emotional intelligence offers a steady compass to navigate the complexity.

Research supports this. Studies have shown that people with higher emotional intelligence are better equipped to handle stress, form lasting relationships, and achieve greater success both personally and professionally. Harvard Business Review calls emotional intelligence "the key to professional success," while research from Yale University's Center for Emotional Intelligence shows that individuals who prioritize emotional well-being are more resilient in times of crisis.

The good news is that emotional intelligence isn't fixed—it can be developed and strengthened over time. The small shifts you make in how you perceive your emotions, how you communicate, and how you engage with others have a compounding effect. Each positive interaction, each thoughtful response, and each moment of empathy adds up, shaping the person you're becoming.

Applying What You've Learned: Key Takeaways

Let's revisit some of the core lessons from this book that you can carry forward into your daily life:

1. **Self-Awareness is the Foundation:** By tuning in to your own emotions, you gain clarity about who you are, what you need, and how your feelings impact your actions. Regularly reflect on your emotional triggers and take note of patterns that emerge. Remember, the more you understand yourself, the better you can guide your actions.
2. **Emotional Regulation is a Skill:** Life is unpredictable, but your emotional responses don't have to be. When you feel overwhelmed, practice grounding techniques like mindfulness, deep breathing, or reframing your thoughts. This allows you to stay centered even in the face of difficulty.
3. **Empathy is Your Superpower:** Understanding others—truly seeing and hearing them—can transform relationships. The next time you're in a disagreement or feel distant from someone, pause. Ask yourself: What might they be feeling? How can I validate their emotions without

compromising my own needs?

4. **Healthy Relationships Require Effort:** Relationships don't thrive on autopilot. They require communication, trust, and emotional investment. Use the tools you've learned to build deeper, more fulfilling connections, whether in your personal or professional life. Remember, relationships are strengthened not just by good times, but by how we handle challenges together.

A Final Thought: Keep Evolving

As you move forward, know that emotional intelligence is a skill set that grows with you. You don't have to master it all at once. Start where you are. Some days, you'll get it right—handling a conflict with grace, offering empathy when it's needed, or staying calm in a stressful moment. Other days, you might struggle. But that's okay.

The goal isn't perfection; it's evolution. Over time, you'll find yourself responding to challenges with greater ease, building relationships that are more authentic, and maintaining a deeper connection with yourself. Emotional intelligence isn't just a tool for success—it's a pathway to a more fulfilled, meaningful life.

Stay Committed to Growth

As you close this book, think about one area of your emotional intelligence that you'd like to focus on. Is it self-awareness? Empathy? Conflict resolution? Whatever it is, commit to making small, intentional changes in your daily life. Reflect on your progress, and celebrate the wins along the way.

Remember, emotional intelligence is a lifelong journey. Embrace it fully, and watch how it transforms not only your relationships but your entire approach to life.

You've got this!!!

Reflection Exercise: A Personal Inventory

Before you finish, take a moment to reflect on the following questions. Write down your answers to solidify your learning:

1. **What is the biggest lesson I've learned about myself through this book?**
2. **Which aspect of emotional intelligence have I already begun to develop?**
3. **What is one relationship in my life where I can apply these lessons?**
4. **How will I continue to nurture my emotional intelligence in the months and years to come?**

Bonus Section: Deepening Your Emotional Intelligence with Practical Exercises

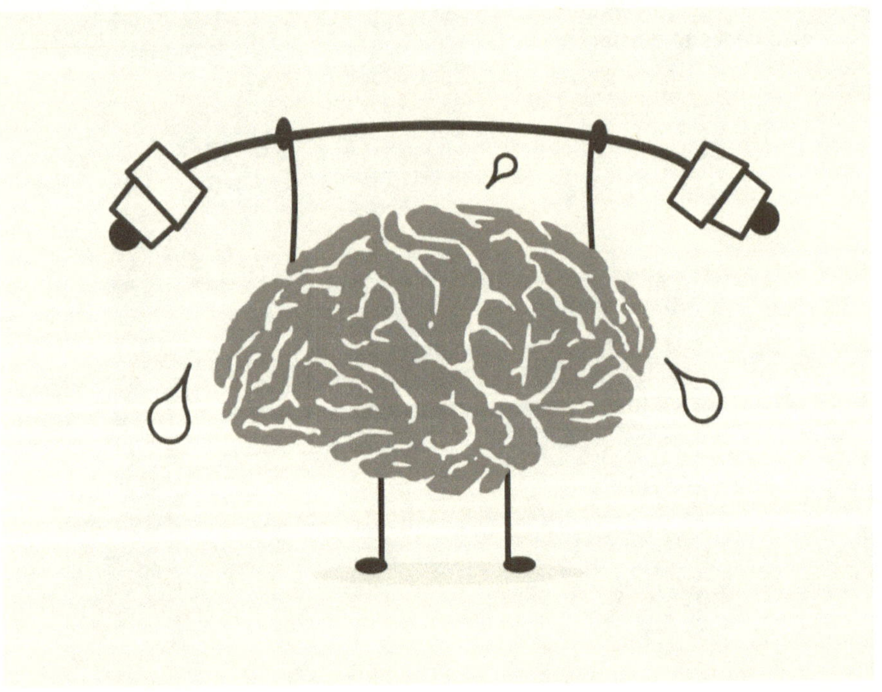

As a final part of this journey, this bonus section is designed to help you take the principles you've learned to a deeper, more personal level. Emotional intelligence is a skill you can cultivate through intentional practice, and these exercises will help you engage in real-life application. Each exercise is crafted to push you beyond surface-level understanding and encourage genuine emotional growth. Let's dive in.

1. The Emotional Audit: A Week of Emotional Self-Awareness

This exercise focuses on self-awareness by helping you recognize and label your emotions throughout your day. The goal is to bring consciousness to your emotional patterns so you can manage them more effectively.

How to Perform the Emotional Audit

Step 1: Set aside 5 minutes at the end of each day for a week to reflect on your emotional experiences.

Step 2: Write down the key emotions you felt throughout the day. Be specific—rather than just "happy" or "angry," use more precise terms like "elated," "frustrated," or "anxious."

Step 3: Identify what triggered these emotions. Was it a particular situation, person, or thought?

Step 4: Reflect on how you reacted to these emotions. Did you respond in a way that aligned with your goals, or did you react impulsively?

Step 5: Journal any patterns you notice at the end of the week. Are there recurring emotions or triggers that you can work on managing more effectively?

The Takeaway

This exercise brings awareness to how emotions impact your daily life. By identifying patterns and understanding what triggers certain emotions, you're better equipped to manage them constructively.

2. The Mirror of Empathy: Developing Deeper Empathy

Empathy is one of the most powerful tools in emotional intelligence. This exercise encourages you to actively practice empathy by putting yourself in someone else's shoes—literally.

How to Practice the Mirror of Empathy

Step 1: Choose someone in your life with whom you have regular interactions. It could be a friend, colleague, or family member. Ideally, pick someone you'd like to understand better.

Step 2: For one week, observe their behavior, emotions, and non-verbal cues closely. Try to imagine what they might be feeling or thinking throughout the day. What pressures or challenges are they facing that might explain their behavior?

Step 3: Write down your observations at the end of each day. Try to pinpoint specific moments when you noticed a strong emotion or reaction from them.

Step 4: At the end of the week, engage in a conversation with this person, focusing on active listening. Rather than offering advice or solutions, listen with the intent to understand.

Step 5: After the conversation, reflect on whether your understanding of their emotions was accurate. How did your perception of their feelings change?

The Takeaway

This exercise will strengthen your ability to empathize with others by actively practicing emotional perspective-taking. It's an opportunity to deepen relationships through more thoughtful communication.

3. The 24-Hour Reaction Challenge: Mastering Emotional Regulation

Regulating your emotions, especially in moments of stress or conflict, is a hallmark of emotional intelligence. This challenge will help you practice controlling emotional reactions and maintaining composure.

How to Perform the 24-Hour Reaction Challenge

Step 1: Choose a day when you expect to face emotional triggers—whether it's a busy workday, a stressful social event, or a personal situation that typically tests your patience.

Step 2: Set a rule for yourself: for 24 hours, you will not immediately react to any negative emotions. Instead, take a brief pause—5 to 10 seconds—before responding to any trigger.

Step 3: During that pause, ask yourself: "What am I feeling right now?" and "How do I want to respond in a way that aligns with my long-term goals?" This pause allows your emotional brain to reset and prevents impulsive reactions.

Step 4: At the end of the day, journal about your experience. Did pausing help you respond more thoughtfully? Were there moments where you struggled to regulate your emotions? What could you do differently next time?

The Takeaway

This challenge cultivates emotional regulation by training your mind to pause before reacting. Over time, this practice helps you build greater control over how you respond to emotional triggers.

4. The Circle of Trust: Strengthening Relationships Through Vulnerability

Trust is the foundation of meaningful relationships, but trust is built through vulnerability and open communication. This exercise encourages you to take a leap of faith by sharing something personal in a relationship you'd like to strengthen.

How to Strengthen Trust Through Vulnerability

Step 1: Choose a person in your life with whom you'd like to strengthen trust. This could be a partner, friend, or colleague.

Step 2: Identify something personal you'd like to share with this person that you haven't shared before. It could be an experience, a fear, a challenge, or even a hope for the future.

Step 3: Set a time to have an open, honest conversation with this person. Share your thoughts or feelings with the intention of being vulnerable, while also creating space for them to share if they feel comfortable.

Step 4: Reflect on how this act of vulnerability impacts your relationship. Did it create a deeper connection? Were you able to communicate more openly than before?

The Takeaway

Vulnerability is a cornerstone of building trust, but it requires courage. This exercise allows you to take small steps toward creating deeper, more meaningful relationships by being open and honest with those you care about.

5. Emotional Intelligence in Action: Role-Playing Scenarios

This exercise is designed to give you hands-on practice in applying emotional intelligence to real-life situations. By role-playing different scenarios, you'll gain confidence in handling tough conversations, managing conflict, and offering support.

How to Use Role-Playing to Practice Emotional Intelligence

Step 1: Identify a real-life scenario that challenges your emotional intelligence. Examples could include:

1. A difficult conversation with a coworker or boss.
2. A tense interaction with a friend or family member.
3. A situation where you need to offer emotional support to someone in distress.

Step 2: Find a partner (a friend or family member) who's willing to role-play the scenario with you.

Step 3: Act out the scenario, practicing the key emotional intelligence skills you've learned: active listening, empathy, emotional regulation, and clear communication.

Step 4: After the role-play, ask your partner for feedback. What did you do well? Where could you improve? Discuss alternative approaches to handling the situation.

Step 5: Reflect on the exercise. How did it feel to use emotional intelligence in a controlled environment? How might you apply these skills in real life?

The Takeaway

Role-playing helps bridge the gap between theory and practice. By simulating real-life interactions, you'll gain greater confidence in using emotional intelligence when it matters most.

6. The Empathy Map: Seeing the World Through Someone Else's Eyes

This exercise is a powerful tool for developing empathy by encouraging you to step outside of your perspective and see the world as someone else experiences it.

How to Create an Empathy Map

Step 1: Choose someone in your life whose emotions you've struggled to understand.

Step 2: On a piece of paper, create four quadrants and label them: "Thinking," "Feeling," "Seeing," and "Doing."

Step 3: In each quadrant, fill in what you believe this person might be thinking, feeling, seeing, and doing on a daily basis. Focus on their challenges, emotional state, and world view.

- **Thinking**: What might be occupying their thoughts? What concerns or goals are they focused on?
- **Feeling**: What emotions might they be experiencing regularly? Are they stressed, joyful, anxious, or excited?
- **Seeing**: What does their daily life look like? What might their environment or relationships look like from their perspective?
- **Doing**: What actions are they taking as a result of their thoughts and feelings? How do they behave in various situations?

Step 4: Use the empathy map as a guide for a conversation with this person. Ask questions that help validate or refine your understanding of their experience.

The Takeaway

The Empathy Map helps you step into someone else's shoes in a structured way, encouraging you to see the world through their eyes. This process deepens your empathy and strengthens your relationships.

7.The "Name It to Tame It" Technique: Mastering Emotional Labeling

This exercise helps you identify and name specific emotions as they arise. Labeling your emotions is a powerful technique for regulating them and reducing their intensity.

How to Practice Emotional Labeling:

- **Step 1**: Throughout your day, take note of moments when you feel a strong emotion—whether positive or negative. It could be joy, frustration, anxiety, or anything else.
- **Step 2**: Instead of simply feeling the emotion, pause for a moment and name it. For example, say to yourself, "I am feeling anxious" or "I am feeling frustrated."
- **Step 3**: After labeling the emotion, ask yourself what triggered it and how intense it feels on a scale of 1 to 10.
- **Step 4**: Reflect on how naming the emotion affects your experience. Does it reduce its intensity? Does it make you more aware of how you're feeling?

The Takeaway

By naming your emotions, you gain more control over them, making it easier to regulate your reactions and make thoughtful decisions.

8. The Gratitude Journal: Boosting Emotional Resilience

Gratitude has been shown to increase positive emotions and overall well-being. This simple journaling exercise will help you focus on the positive aspects of your life, cultivating a mindset of gratitude.

How to Start a Gratitude Journal:

- **Step 1**: At the end of each day, write down three things that you are grateful for. These can be big or small, such as a kind interaction with a colleague, a delicious meal, or a moment of personal achievement.
- **Step 2**: After listing the three things, reflect on how they made you feel

and why they matter to you. This reflection helps deepen the emotional impact of gratitude.

- **Step 3**: Continue this practice daily for at least one week, and notice how your overall emotional state shifts over time.

The Takeaway

Practicing gratitude helps shift your focus from negative emotions to positive ones, increasing your emotional resilience and overall happiness.

9. The Relationship Check-In: Strengthening Communication and Connection

This exercise encourages regular, open communication with people close to you, helping to maintain and deepen your relationships.

How to Perform a Relationship Check-In:

- **Step 1**: Choose a person with whom you want to strengthen your relationship—this could be a partner, friend, or family member.
- **Step 2**: Set aside time once a week for a relationship check-in, where you both talk openly about your feelings, needs, and any concerns.
- **Step 3**: Use active listening during the check-in—focus on truly hearing the other person without interrupting or offering advice unless asked.
- **Step 4**: Reflect on how these conversations make you feel and how they impact your connection with the other person.

The Takeaway

Regular check-ins promote emotional openness and understanding, which are key to building and maintaining healthy, emotionally intelligent relationships.

10. The Emotional Time Machine: Reflection for Future Growth

This visualization exercise encourages you to reflect on how past emotional experiences have shaped your growth and how you want to apply emotional intelligence moving forward.

How to Use the Emotional Time Machine:

- **Step 1**: Find a quiet space where you can sit comfortably without distraction.
- **Step 2**: Close your eyes and think back to a time when you handled a difficult emotion, like anger or sadness. What triggered that emotion? How did you react? What did you learn from that experience?
- **Step 3**: Now, imagine yourself in the future—five or ten years from now. Visualize a version of yourself who has fully developed emotional intelligence. How do you handle challenges and relationships in this future version of your life?
- **Step 4**: Reflect on what steps you can take today to move closer to that future version of yourself. Write down one or two actions you can commit to in order to grow emotionally.

The Takeaway

Reflecting on both past and future emotional experiences helps you understand how far you've come and where you still want to grow. It provides clarity on what actions you can take to become the person you envision.

Keep Practicing

These exercises are designed to help you go beyond theory and bring emotional intelligence into your everyday life. Just like any other skill, emotional intelligence grows stronger with practice. You may not get it right every time, but each small step you take adds up to lasting improvement.

Challenge yourself to practice one of these exercises each week, and observe how your emotional awareness, relationships, and overall well-being evolve over time. Remember, emotional intelligence isn't a one-time effort—it's a lifelong journey of growth and self-discovery.